To: Con

From:

Rayceni

May 2014

Functioning in the Apostolic

Apostle Fannie M. Wallace

WestBow
PRESS
A DIVISION OF THOMAS NELSON

WestBow Press books may be ordered through booksellers or by contacting:

WestBow Press
A Division of Thomas Nelson
1663 Liberty Drive
Bloomington, IN 47403
www.westbowpress.com
1-(866) 928-1240

For more information, contact Impact Word Ministry,
Apostle Fannie M. Wallace, 3540 SE 15th St., Del City,
OK, 73115, 405-677-3553, www.paafmi.org.

All scriptures are from the King James Version, unless noted otherwise.

With the permission from Apostle John Eckhardt, there are
excerpts from his books, Moving in the Apostolic and Ordinary
People, Extraordinary Power. Thank you, Apostle.

ISBN: 978-1-4497-8212-2 (sc)

Library of Congress Control Number: 2013900741

Printed in the United States of America

WestBow Press rev. date: 2/7/2013

Contents

Preface

This book is written in obedience to God and with the leading of the Holy Spirit who has been my teacher, guide and helper in building this Apostolic Ministry. He taught me all things so that the mandate He had for me would be confirmed, and He called me to bring restoration of the book of Acts (the work of the Apostles), spoken by the prophets. Acts 3: 19-21, "Repent ye therefore, and be converted, that your sins may be blotted out, so that times of refreshing may come from presence of the Lord, and that He may send Jesus Christ, who was preached to you before, whom heaven must receive until the times of restoration of all things, which God has spoken by the mouth of all His Holy prophets since the world began." I thank God that my destiny is being fulfilled in obeying the call as an Apostolic Reformer, and I now am seeing the hunger of pastors who are moving into the function of the Apostolic. I pray the reading of this book will be a blessing unto you and will be a demonstration of the power of the Holy Spirit.

Introduction

When God called us to build a church, He spoke very clearly as to why He called us and what kind of church to build. He spoke to me and said, "Because of your search for the truth and your hunger to know me, you found me. Now with your boldness, I want you to build a latter day church of holiness and righteousness with no compromising of my word." I said, "God, you've got to help us because all we know is we're going to obey." We started a Bible study in our home in August 1993 and with the help of the Holy Spirit who teaches you all things, the hearts of the people changed. Traditional believers were getting filled with the Holy Spirit with the evidence of speaking in tongues.

In September of 1993, God moved on our hearts and thrusted us in building the church that would please Him, rather than man. He confirmed it by sending me to a building that he said would be for rent, and in finding favor with the landlord within a week on September 19, 1993, we had our first Sunday service with 50 chairs, a karaoke machine, and 13 people in attendance. We were not discouraged that even some of those who had been attending the Bible study didn't come because we believed if God called us, He would send those to fulfill the vision. For where there is a vision, God will make provision. God had told me many will come and go, "but I'll never leave you or forsake you." He gave us the name Praise Assembly Full Gospel Ministries because praise and worship had become a lifestyle for me. Believing that "with His stripes I was healed" is what delivered me from sickness of hypochondria that I suffered from for years. That's why I knew the power of praise and worship.

He gave us Ephesians 4:11-16 as our ministry scripture and vision. As the people began to come and we began to teach on holiness, righteousness and speaking in tongues, there was much opposition and accusations coming from the religious and traditional churches and people, so we knew we were moving into the plan and purpose of God that the enemy didn't like. Being taught and led by the Holy Spirit, God would not allow us to be connected to any covering that didn't know His plan for the ministry He called for us to establish. He said the Holy Ghost would teach me all things for He had been given the plan, or blue print. Our challenge was to have a vision of the body of Christ coming together as one in Him as Ephesians 4:13 says, "Til we all come in the unity of the faith, and of the knowledge of the son of God, unto a perfect man, unto the measure of the stature of the fullness of Christ."

After seven years of teaching and preaching and seeing the demonstration of God's power changing people's lives and giving hope for a future, I knew that we were called to be different and separate from the traditional, lukewarm, compromising, comfortable business-as-usual church. Being accused of being a cult church, we weren't accepted by the local pastors.

In March 2000, we were sought out and offered a church that was being resolved as the pastor was retiring, and they had been watching how our ministry was growing, but they would not be able to finance us through their mortgage company because we were not of that denomination. My bank at the time wouldn't give us a loan, so we believed God for a miracle, and shifted our praise toward the church every service. One day I saw an advertisement in a magazine about an apostolic/prophetic conference in Michigan, and I heard the Lord say go. He told me twice to go. Elder Pat, my administrator and armor bearer, and I went to the conference in obedience not knowing anyone there. That first night, a prophet spoke a word confirming to me to obey and give an offering of $1,000 in faith for the church, and I was the first to run down. On the next morning at around 10 am, the president and finance manager called Elder Pat's phone to ask me to come in when we got back to talk to them about financing the church. Glory!

In the meantime at the conference, prophets were releasing and confirming the apostolic gift and anointing on my life everywhere I went. They were recognizing me as an apostle, even on the elevator. I was invited to the apostolic hospitality room where I met Apostle John Eckhardt and after talking with him, he confirmed me to be the first woman apostle who would be effective in my territory.

A prophetic team from Crusaders Ministries of Apostle Eckhardt came to our church, but since I had been teaching on the prophetic and had activated prophets, they confirmed even more the Apostolic anointing that was flowing in our house. In the meantime, God worked favor through man and after five months of waiting and believing in God and obedience to go to that conference, the mortgage holder agreed to finance the church, which was the first time they had ever financed outside of their denomination. That's apostolic!

We paraded over to our new church and on September 19, 2000, we had our first service and everything increased, for God blessed as He enlarged our tent (Isaiah 54:1-3). We acquired the church with everything left in it, fully equipped including a large sanctuary, an abundance of rooms and offices, a daycare, a gym, three houses, and a van. We possessed the land.

A company of apostles confirmed the functioning of

the Apostolic Ministry and in 2001, I was ordained as an apostle. That confirmation released us into the full realm of the apostolic functioning of the latter day ministry. I pray this book will help you understand how it will take apostolic reformation and restoration ministry to fulfill the eternal plan of the Lord. It's apostolic transition time.

Apostles First

I Corinthians 12:28, "God hath set in the church, first apostles, secondarily prophets, thirdly teachers."

Ephesians 4:11, "And He gave some, apostles; and some, prophets; and some, evangelists; and some, pastors and teachers."

Apostles are called, gifted and sent by God, even if they don't know it at first. He is a God that sets things in order. Apostles are given authority to set things in order, which can sometimes mean rebuking, correcting, to even excommunicating because of non-tolerance of sin. It also includes taking authority, dealing with rebellion, disobedience, confusion, strife, division and carnality, which is the flesh that manifests among the saints. To begin with, the Greek word, *proton,* means "first in time, place, order or importance." God is restoring the gift of the apostles that the tradition of men tried to remove.

Mark 7:13, "Making the words of God of none effect through your tradition." This ministry gift has been overlooked because it wasn't being taught; the book of Acts was totally ignored. Apostles and Apostolic Ministry must be recognized as God's order to receive the fullness of its functions and purpose.

Ephesians 4:12-13, "For the perfecting of the saints, for the work of the ministry, for the edifying of the body of Christ: Till we all come in the unity of the faith, and of the knowledge of the Son of God, unto a perfect man, unto the measure of the stature of the fullness of Christ." Prophets, evangelists, pastors and teachers are all needed to bring unity to the body of Christ, but none of these gifts carry the same mandate that the apostle does. A mandate is a command or an order. Apostles are mandated to preach the uncompromised word of God. In I Corinthians 9:16, Paul says, "Woe is me, if I preach not the gospel." Apostles recognize their obligation to fulfill their heavenly mandate. The mandate gives them the drive to persist and persevere in spite of opposition.

The Greek word for apostle is *apostolos* meaning "one sent forth." Therefore, apostles are sent to build, oversee, plant, pull up, water, encourage, correct, activate, pioneer, teach, preach, impart, impact, establish, rule, judge, and release. The apostle carries a breakthrough anointing for the advancement of the kingdom. The word apostle is not a title. It's a function. Because apostles are sent and ordained in the spirit by God, they are determined to not only fulfill their purpose, but also to help those who've been sent and assigned to them whether those areas are cities, regions or nations. Apostles are anointed and have the ability as generals and commanders to mobilize the saints for war and rally the people to work together and accomplish what they've been sent to do. They are given the necessary grace, charisma and wisdom to lead people to whom God called them to be. Apostles set things in order through preaching and teaching of sound doctrine of truth. John 8:32, "And ye shall know the truth, and the truth shall make you free."

Apostles see past all the limitations that come to stop or hinder the establishment of the Apostolic Ministry. They are graced with an authority to confront and defeat the enemy with a spirit of boldness and tenacity. Apostles should be known for their character as well as their action, which includes integrity, courage, strength, honesty, goodness, truthfulness, respectability and morality. Character is what validates the Apostolic Ministry. It is the badge, sign, seal, mark, trademark, stamp and true evidence of an apostle. The seal of a true apostle will be when the believers are birthed and raised into maturity through their ministry. A seal is an embossed emblem, symbol, or letter giving evidence of true authenticity. The apostolic seal authenticates the ministry of a true apostle. That seal is also upon those who follow them. They carry these distinguishing marks as apostolic believers. The seal distinguishes the true from the false.

Apostles are often persecuted, faced with lies and false accusations that come to assassinate their character. In building the ministry, the enemy has been assigned so many times to attack me and the apostolic work with persecution and lies coming from inside the ministry and outside because I refuse to compromise with sin and tradition.

People who were blessed with possessions that they never had before, such as houses, cars, food, clothing, jobs and paid bills, left the church lying to justify their actions. Pastors were coming around our church building praying against me, but in and through it all, God was for me, and He was greater in me than the enemy was against me. I had to walk in the spirit and still show love and not yield to the attacks because I knew in whom I trust and believe. Colossians 1:10, "That ye might walk worthy of the Lord unto all pleasing, being fruitful in every good work, and increasing in the knowledge of God."

Romans 12:9-14 (NIV) "Love must be sincere. Hate what is evil; cling to what is good. Be devoted to one another in brotherly love, honor one another above yourselves. Never be lacking in zeal, but keep your spiritual fervor, serving the Lord. Be joyful in hope, patient in affliction, faithful in prayer. Share with God's people who are in need. Practice hospitality. Bless those who persecute you; bless and do not curse."

The Anointing of an Apostle

1. Apostles must have the "in spite of" anointing and know that their character and integrity is more important than trying to get vengeance and it's just being tested. Romans 12:18-21, "If it be possible as much as lieth in you, live peaceably with all men. Dearly beloved, avenge not yourselves, but rather give place unto wrath: for it is written, vengeance is mine; I will repay saith the Lord. Therefore if thine enemy hunger, feed him; if he thirst, give him drink: for in so doing thou shalt heap coals of fire on his head. Be not overcome of evil, but overcome evil with good." Apostles will be tested in the fire, but God has given them grace to overcome and the anointing to lift the burden.

2. Apostles are *revelators* of the mysteries of God's word, which means they are anointed to unlock the hidden truth of the Bible through the law of impartation. Apostles are defensive of the gospel. They have supernatural passion to defend and be faithful to the truth. Their preaching and teaching will bring fresh strength to the church.

3. Apostles are anointed and passionate to see the spiritual gifts in others stirred up and activated and manifested to fulfill their purpose. Second Timothy 6: "That thou stir up the gift of God, which is in thee." Signs and

wonders, miracles, healing and deliverance should be demonstrated through the taught word and life of an apostle, while advancing the kingdom of God. Acts 5:12, "And by the hands of the apostles were many signs and wonders wrought among the people." First Corinthians 2:4, "And my speech and my preaching was not with enticing words of man's wisdom, but in demonstration of the spirit of power."

4. Apostles are reformers who have the ability to pull down the strong holds of tradition by bringing the church into proper apostolic order. The word *reform* means "to amend, make changes, improve, make right, renovate, rectify, correct." This takes the anointing of an apostle.

5. Apostles are forerunners. Jesus sent them out with authority. (Luke 10:1) Apostles are also ambassadors, an official delegate to go in representation of a greater assignment. They speak for others. Apostles can evangelize, prophesy, teach, preach and pastor. Although there might be a greater dimension of one of the other, they can flow in each if they ask God. His grace is sufficient. First Corinthians 12:31, "But covet earnestly the best gifts: and yet show I unto you a more excellent way." I remember when I began to teach on the different gifts of the spirit. I prayed and asked God to anoint me with all the gifts of the Holy Spirit to equip me and the people to fulfill what He

called us to do in the latter day. This anointing also gives the ability to impart revelation to the church, which becomes the foundation on which the church is built.

6. Apostles are anointed to be pioneers and planters, sometimes being the first to enter into new regions birthing apostolic work. To *pioneer* means "to advance, progress, conquer territory, gain ground, establish, and start." Apostles are anointed to break through all obstacles that keep people and the advancement of the move of the apostolic from operating.

7. Apostles are anointed to pray without ceasing, warfaring for global manifestation of the apostolic. Acts 6:4, "But we will give ourselves continually to prayer and to the ministry of the word."

8. Apostles carry a certain amount of grace to release the anointing given to them. This is the law of impartation. The release of this anointing will bring blessings, miracles, healing and deliverance. The apostle has received an anointing to release because they received a measure from Christ to impart to the saints.

9. Apostles are anointed to convert people to the laws and apostolic culture of the kingdom. Apostolic culture is a spiritual culture, not carnal or traditional, so mindsets must change to embrace the teaching of kingdom culture.

10. Apostles are anointed to execute, complete and fulfill the plans of God, spoken by the prophets.

11. Apostles are anointed to be spiritual fathers/mothers. They birth, protect, teach and mentor. 1 Corinthians 4:15-16. They ordain and appoint elders and apostles and oversee, mentor and cover their apostolic work. God is gracing the reforming apostolic church with the anointing that is needed to build the church that the gates of hell cannot prevail. Therefore, there are pastors who are crying out and receiving the apostolic mandate to shift from the pastoral to the anointing of an apostle.

12. Apostles are anointed with passion to see the kingdom of God manifesting on earth through the apostolic believers' demonstration of the power of the Holy Spirit.

Apostolic Function

The word of the Lord tells us of a restoration of all things before the return of the Lord. We are seeing the restoration of the apostolic church. Scriptures declare the word "whom the heaven must receive until times of restoration of all things which God hath spoken by the mouth of all His holy prophets since the world began" according to Acts 3:21. We have entered that time of restoration, but you can't have time of restoration without times of reformation. To *reform* means "to improve, make better, change, remake, renovate, rectify or correct." The spirit of reformation is the spirit of change. Change is uncomfortable but necessary to build the latter day church. A paradigm shift is causing change in how ministry is being built. A *paradigm* is "a model, a pattern or a way of thinking or mindset." In this paradigm shift, God is realigning and restructuring the church, so leaders must transition for the latter day work of the Apostolic Ministry.

Many leaders are sensing the call to shift from pastoral thinking to apostolic thinking. They are hearing a sound of release to transition. There is a greater call for embracing apostolic functioning. To *shift* means "to move from one place to another, change position, to be replaced by another." I am meeting pastors who are hearing the clarion call and are ready to answer. After years of traditional, denominational churching, they are feeling a void and are tired of dry, mundane ministry. They are realizing their lives and their members are not being fulfilled because something is missing. I hear the statement "I need more" all the time. Many of these pastors are crying out for help or they are ready to shut it all down. Thank God for the restoration of the apostolic ministry. Many pastors have been introduced to the apostolic ministry, but are fearful of the shift. They are not sure what the members will do, whether they will shift with them or shift out from them. They will find that they can't fulfill an apostolic calling with a pastoral mindset because it limits them and keeps them church and people-minded instead of God and kingdom-minded. I am not saying every pastor is an apostle, but every pastor should function apostolically. The word *function* means "to be in action, work, to operate and perform." There are a lot of leaders who are calling themselves apostles, but there is no apostolic manifestation. They desire the name, but they are not producing the work. To Paul, an apostle was a function, not a title (2 Corinthians 12:12). There is an apostolic mandate releasing pastors and church leadership to be free to operate in their higher calling and gifts of God. The church is experiencing great breakthroughs with apostolic leadership.

This shift results in changes in ministry function with greater manifestations of signs, wonders, power, wisdom, revelations and a release of ministry gifts, (Ephesians 4:8). Paul states that Christ gave these gifts for (1) The equipping of God's people for the work of service and (2) for the spiritual growth and development of the body of Christ as God had planned. The apostolic anointing functions in a greater dimension than the pastoral. (1) The apostolic anointing meets the needs of the people by exhorting them to pursue their divine purpose. (2) The apostolic anointing challenges the people to trust God to supply their needs through relationship with him, not expecting the pastor to do everything for them. (3) The apostolic anointing mandate brings a greater flow of revelation into the people's lives, so they will be able to do what God is calling them to do. (4) The apostolic anointing doesn't just maintain the people, but mature the people for purpose. (5) The apostolic anointing gives grace to shift believers for kingdom advancement, imparting gifts to function. (6) The apostolic anointing releases greater power and authority to bind and loose. (7) The apostolic anointing sets things in order with strong correction and rebuking with love. (8) The apostolic anointing carries all that is needed to build and fulfill the end-times commission. (9) The apostolic anointing has the power and authority to destroy and cast out the power of darkness. (10) The apostolic anointing keeps you moving forward with the ability to overcome obstacles that are there to stop you from fulfilling your purpose.

God is calling on an apostolic reformation to execute the plan of the last days, and He is releasing an end-time apostolic mandate. Reformation is a radical process, a time of revolutionary change. Leadership is being forced to change for the sake of the kingdom. The kingdom of God is at hand (Mark 1:15). The Lord sends for apostles when there is need for reformation. Reformation brings order and apostles are anointed to bring the church in proper order. The enemy doesn't want order in the church, so he uses the weapon of fear for some pastors who desire to change. Reformation is not new, but is being restored by pastors who are seeing the need to shift into apostolic functioning. For those pastors who are ready to fulfill the call of God on their lives now. For these emerging pastors who are ready for apostolic reformation, they must be ready to connect to a functioning apostle to be encouraged and trained to fulfill their destiny as well as those that have been sent to them to fulfill their destiny. Apostolic functioning is necessary to build the latter day church that Jesus will return to. After teaching for some years on the apostolic ministry releasing gifts and establishing the church, we began to see the manifestation of the teaching. Prophets were released. Pastoral anointing was imparted and received. All five-fold ministry gifts began to flow and brought spiritual increase. As a result, the church began to see all kinds of miracles in the house. There was demonstration of God's power through the laying on of hands, deliverance, and prayer that confirmed we are true apostolic people. After being confirmed in 2007, God gave us a name change to Praise Assembly Apostolic Faith Ministries International and has given us the mandate as an "apostolic hub," center of spirit-filled activity. There is always movement and action and manifestation of apostolic functioning. In 19 years of ministry, there has never been the same routine, ritual service. The Holy Spirit moves His way to meet the needs of the people and manifests signs, wonders, deliverance, healing.

We have seen the power of God through the laying on of hands on the sick and they recovered. One demonstration was when Pastor Pat stopped breathing, and God instructed me to sprinkle water in her face three times (Father, Son and Holy Ghost). She opened her eyes and started breathing again. After three days in bed and my obedience to God, she recovered. Mrs. Ruby had two brain aneurisms and God said she would recover all, and she is a testimony of being in an apostolic ministry who believes in miracles. Elder Wesley was diagnosed with a brain-bleeding stroke, and although the doctor said he wouldn't make it through the night, the prayers of the righteous went forth and within two months, he returned back to church on his post as a porter. Many testimonies of blessings and increase have manifested to confirm the word of God at Praise Assembly Apostolic Faith Ministries International.

An apostolic church should function in every dimension of a sent ministry to fulfill the latter day commission. Matthew 28: 19, 20, "Go therefore and make disciples of all the nation, baptizing them in the name of the Father and of the Son and of the Holy Spirit, teaching them to observe all things that I have commanded you; and lo, I am with you always, even to the end of the age. Amen."

This apostolic commission is for today, and it must be fulfilled through the reforming of the Apostolic Ministry of Apostles.

Apostolic Administration

According to 1 Corinthians 12:28, there are two vitally important gifts that are necessary in building an apostolic ministry. The gift of helps and government is a supportive ministry. These gifts are given to those who have the grace to embrace the vision of the apostles and help to bring the plans and purposes of God to pass. Although some apostles have good administrative abilities, to have someone that has the gift would release them to focus on the big picture of the vision, while the administration carries it out. Administrators must be anointed with strength and gifted to organize, delegate and direct the people to fulfill the vision that God has given the apostle. Administration helps get the work done without bringing a hardship on the apostle by working out the details, whether large or small, without frustration. They help and teach the people how to help. They should be visionary people to see what the apostle sees in order to be in agreement with what God is doing. They should have a heart for God, a heart for ministry and a heart for the apostle. Anointed administrators will be the bridge between the people and the apostles. They take to the people the directions and vision and delegate how to bring it to pass. They should never appear to be in disagreement with what they are asked to do before the people. Because of the influence of the administration, the apostle must trust that they won't take advantage of the people on a personal level, and the people should be able to trust that the apostle is aware of what they are asked to do. The gift is to take the load off the apostle, not to be the load or the problem.

Churches can rise or fall because of the strength, commitment and dedication of the administration of the ministry. Building an apostolic ministry without the help of administration is like building a house without a foundation. It is governmental, setting all the other areas of ministry up to properly work. When we birthed the ministry, we knew we didn't want the traditional organization of church.

At the time of our ministry birthing, the only adults were my husband, Pastor William, Pastor Pat Jenkins, my sister-in-law and myself, so of course we had to depend on the Holy Spirit to teach us everything. Since Pastor Pat had worked for the state Secretary/Administration, this area of ministry became her focus. As the pastor, I didn't have the full vision, but as God gave it to us, she was there to help carry it out. Even at the time, we didn't know we were Apostolic. I've always believed in doing things in excellence, so there were certain expectations I had when it came to how I wanted things done. Pastor Pat had been in church leadership for many years, but we had to work putting things in proper order because what worked for that ministry was not this vision. One thing is for sure, she was sent to help fulfill the vision for Praise Assembly because through faith and prayer, it began to work. The mandate of administrator was given to her, and we released her in that gift to help support where God was leading us. She also serves as my armor bearer to help and support my personal needs.

With her having the gift to facilitate the vision of administration, I was able to focus on studying, praying, and teaching the people what the Holy Spirit was teaching me. She has been effectively positioned as administrator from the beginning to now. Every emerging apostle needs to pray for an administrator with a heart for the gift to help build Apostolic Ministry effectively.

Apostolic Ministry
of Deliverance

Apostolic Ministry must be spiritually equipped in deliverance ministry to help people break free from unclean work of the flesh. Jesus gave His disciples power against unclean spirits, and we need to have that same power to cast them out now. Matthew 10:1, "And when He had called unto Him His twelve disciples, He gave them power against unclean spirits, to cast them out." Demons are manifested through generations, lifestyles, rebellion, and environment, many ways assigned by the devil to keep people in bondage in the natural and in the spirit. Coming into Apostolic Ministry, most people will need deliverance in order to get free to receive truth, walk in the spirit, and trust in the word of God. Deliverance is necessary to expose sin, opening up the way to keep holiness in the church. Deliverance frees and releases people to fulfill their destiny. I remember when we first started the ministry, we didn't really know what we were doing, but every Sunday night, it seemed that we had demonic forces coming in. I had done some deliverance at my previous church, but we were getting some hard-core witchcraft, sexual, religious, and controlling spirits showing up. The Holy Spirit gave us the spiritual strategies on how to call out the demonic force of darkness, to rule and reign over demons, and people were getting free. We were being talked about being a cult, but you couldn't come in Praise Assembly and operate in witchcraft or any other demonic force. Like Jesus, the Chief Apostle, apostles are sent to destroy the works of the devil.

1 John 3:8b, "For this purpose the Son of God was manifested, that he might destroy the works of the devil." The company of prophets at Praise Assembly is also the deliverance team ministry and many captives have been set free and are now walking in their purpose.

Apostolic Spiritual Warfare

Apostolic people are people of warfare because of the spiritual conflict that they are faced with. The enemy hates apostolic ministry, so there is always opposition to stop the work. Apostolic churches are called to pull down strongholds.

2 Corinthians 10:4-5, "For the weapons of our warfare are not carnal (fleshly), but mighty through God to the pulling down of strongholds; Casting down imaginations, and every high thing that exalteth itself against the knowledge of God, and bringing into captivity every thought to the obedience of Christ." Ephesians 6:12, 18, "For we wrestle not against flesh and blood, but against principalities, against powers, against the rulers of the darkness of this world, against spiritual wickedness in high places…Praying always with all prayer and supplication in

the Spirit, and watching thereunto with all perseverance and supplication for all saints."

Apostolic people are always engaged in spiritual conflict with evil warfare. In 2 Corinthians 10:4 is the Greek word *stateia*, which means "apostolic career (one of hardship and danger)." Strongholds are influences that keep people from the knowledge of God and prevent them from obeying the truth. Ignorance and rebellion are the result. These are usually people whose mind is set not to receive apostolic ministry. Because of their ignorance, carnal people would rather argue that this ministry has ceased. Apostolic warfare people have the anointing and ability to confront and pull down these strongholds.

Apostolic ministry has the power and authority to destroy strongholds and change mindsets that oppose the truth. Apostolic prayer warriors must pray to see territorial change. They must pray for changes in churches, government, families, and schools and for the salvation of the souls. Apostolic churches should warfare in prayer two to three times a week to release angels to help break through the power of darkness of the region.

Apostolic Intercession

The power of apostolic prayer and intercession will release the captives and set them free. With the whole church in intercession, sudden changes take place. In Acts 12:5, the apostles and the New Testament believers were facing persecution, but they fervently prayed. The situation they faced looked impossible to change with James already dead and Herod had Peter in the custody of 16 men, but the church prayed intensely and continuously over Peter's situation, and their intercession was suddenly answered (Acts 12: 6-17).

James 5:16, "The effectual fervent prayers of the righteous man availed much." Apostolic churches should be called the House of Prayer pleading with God on behalf of others who need an intervention from God. Jesus prayed in intercession for the multitudes, his disciples, and his enemies.

Luke 19:10, "For the Son of man is come to seek and to save that which was lost."

Luke 22:32, "But I have prayed for thee, that thy faith fail not: and when thou art converted, strengthen thy brethren."

Luke 23:34, "Then said Jesus, Father, forgive them; for they know not what they do. And they parted his raiment, and cast lots." There are many times in the Bible where intercessory prayer was prayed and God intervened. Moses prayed on behalf of the Israelites who rebelled against God and refused to go into Canaan. God was going to destroy them, but Moses prayed and pleaded for them and at the end of his prayer, God heard and answered his prayer (Numbers 14:1-20). God still hears the prayer of faith, so the church must continue in prayer according to the will of God. Corporate prayer of intercession is powerful enough to release angels to break through the power of darkness. Apostolic believers should be filled with the Holy Spirit, with the evidence of speaking in tongues. Praying in the spirit helps you pray in the supernatural beyond the limitations of your understanding. When praying in the spirit, the spirit knows what to pray for (Romans 8:26-27). Apostolic churches must focus on prayer to neutralize the powers of hell that hate the ministry of the apostolic and also hinder the people from receiving breakthrough.

Apostolic Praise

Apostolic churches should demonstrate high praise of celebration. This dimension of praise releases the anointing to pull down strongholds, set the atmosphere for God's glory to enter into the presence of His people. There is liberty through praise in apostolic churches with dancing, shouting, clapping, leaping in thanksgiving of His goodness.

Psalms 147, "Praise ye the Lord, for it is good to sing praises unto our God: for it is pleasant and praise is comely, pleasing in appearance."

Psalms 149:2-3, 6-9, "Praise ye the Lord, sing unto the Lord a new song and His praise in the congregation of saints. Let the children of Zion be joyful in their king. Let them praise His name in the dance; let them sing praises unto Him with the timbrel and harp...Let the high praises of God be their mouth and a two-edged sword in their hand; To execute vengeance upon the heathen, and punishments upon the people; To bind their kings with chains, and their nobles with fetters of iron; To execute upon them the judgment written; this honor have all saints. Praise ye the Lord."

Praise will oppose Satan's kingdom and all his evil devices; therefore, as you praise, the anointing is released to warfare against the weapon of the enemy. At Praise Assembly, we sing a song entitled "My Praise is My Weapon." All opposing forces must be pulled down at the sound of praise. Anointed praise destroys the yokes as the presence of the Lord is being released. God does not need our praise. We need to praise Him. He inhabits our praise. He moves in the midst of apostolic praise. Praise is a lifestyle, not a ritual. It builds our faith as we build our relationship with God. Like David, you need to make it personal: "I will bless the Lord at all times: His praise shall continually be in my mouth," (Psalms 34:1). Praise is a choice and David made a choice to bless Him whether he felt like it or not. Sometimes you just have to tell yourself, "I will bless the Lord no matter what I'm going through, not because I feel like it, it's because He's worthy." Praise is an expression, and expression has a sound. Praise is action (dance, lifted hands, clap, leap, jump). Psalms 95, "O come, let us sing unto the Lord; let us make a joyful noise to the rock of our salvation. Let us come before His presence with thanksgiving and make a joyful noise unto Him with psalms. For the Lord is a great God, and a great king above all gods." *Noise* means "unwanted sound," and the devil doesn't want to hear the sound of a praiser because when you exhort God, you are denying the devil and his power. I meet people who say they want more praise in their church because they are used to a ritual of two praise and possibly two worship songs, which might last a total of thirty minutes. But then they come to Praise Assembly and experience the Holy Ghost move of apostolic praise and worship. They can't believe that the anointing will cause breakthroughs, healing, deliverance, and God's glory is released through exhortation and prophetic songs. That's why you can't build an apostolic church by singing traditional hymns and songs that have nothing to do with honoring God. Praise taps you into the presence of God, and worship keeps you in His presence where there is fullness of joy.

As I said before, praise is a lifestyle, and when we develop a lifestyle of praise, it builds our faith so that when we are called upon to step out in faith, it's there for us. We have to maintain our praise no matter what. The church experienced this in 2000 when we were waiting for the final decision of the church we were offered to buy. While waiting every service, we would praise and shout "shift" as we pointed toward the direction of the church. The night they were to meet, before our service was over that day, we were aware that it was predicted to rain, but God told me to tell the people to come back to night service to praise and shift. God had connected me to one of their deacons as my divine connector. He was the one who came to offer us the church and was in favor of us to possess it. On our way back to church, it rained and flooded the streets, and although some of the people's cars stopped in the floods, they walked in the rain with children and were soaked. We praised God and shouted "shift" until after midnight, and I felt a release. The next morning in trying to reach the deacon, we were having telephone difficulties, so I went to meet Him to ask what the decision was. He told me, "For a while it looked like no go, but all of a *sudden* things turned." He said, "It was probably while you all were doing all that praise that the voting went your way." I tell you praise will give you the victory in warfare and give God the glory for what He's done. I know that God was in the midst of our sacrifice of praise. Psalms 67:5, "Let the people praise thee, O God; let all the people praise thee. Then shall the earth yield her increase; and God, even our own God shall bless us."

Hebrews 13:15, "By Him therefore let us offer the sacrifice of praise to God continually, that is, the fruit of our lips giving thanks to His name." Psalms 107:22, "And let them sacrifice the sacrifices of thanksgiving and declare His works with rejoicing."

Apostolic ministries should be the center of high praise in celebration of the Lord who has brought us out of darkness into His marvelous light. Some people would tell me "It don't take all that" when they would see me praising God, but I'd tell them, "You weren't there when God did what He did for me. He deserves praise from me, maybe not you."

Apostolic Worship

Apostolic worshippers love the presence of God, from where they draw their strength. Worship takes place in spirit and truth. As Jesus said to the woman at the well, you can't worship Him in the flesh, but you must be spiritually connected to Him as your God. John 4:23-24, "But the hour cometh, and now is when the true worshippers shall worship the Father in spirit and in truth; for the father seeketh such to worship Him." God is a spirit; and they that worship Him must worship Him in spirit and in truth. Worship must take place according to God's revelation of Himself and the Son. The hour is now for God to be reverenced and honored for His greatness, with thanksgiving for what He has done for us in Christ through the Holy Spirit. Worship is God-centered, not man-centered. For who He is, He deserves the worship. Psalms 29:1, "Give unto the Lord, O ye mighty, give unto the Lord glory and strength. Give unto the Lord, the glory due unto His name; worship the Lord in the beauty of holiness." Apostolic people are worshippers. Apostles are anointed to establish a spirit of worship. Some are anointed to lead the presence of the Lord into the atmosphere as they exhort, sing prophetic songs, giving God the glory. With an open heaven, the Lord pours His blessings upon the people. Healing, deliverance, and freedom take place. The apostolic provides an atmosphere of His glory for His people to come into His presence and be changed. When the glory of God manifests through worship at Praise Assembly, the church at large experiences "floorology." In other words, worship bows the people prostrate to the floor, giving reverence to the awesomeness of the presence of the Lord.

I grew up in a traditional church, and I always sung in the choir, directed choirs, and lead solos in church. When I had an experience with God at a youth conference at 15-years-old, I began to have a void in my life. I knew that there was more for me than singing, but traditional pastors kept telling me women didn't preach so keep singing. So for 30 years I had a void for more of God. When I got filled with the Holy Spirit in 1988, I sought all of God. I hungered and thirsted for his presence, just to know Him and His presence. At that time, I was in recovery of a back injury. I would spend hours in worship at home. It was during this time that God healed my back because all of a sudden, the pain was gone. Praise God, worship became a lifestyle for me, and God became personal to me, which is relationship. Worship is vital in the lives of apostolic people and apostolic churches. When true worship of David is restored to the church, we will see changes in the nations and the harvest will be saved.

The Prophetic

The Lord is raising up the Prophetic Voice in the last days for the advancement of the kingdom of God. Restoration of the prophetic ministry is necessary to help build the foundation of apostolic ministry. Ephesians 4:11 lists the ministry gift of prophets, which Christ gave to the church for the equipping of the saints for service for the spiritual growth and development of the body of Christ. 1 Corinthians 14:29-32, "Let the prophets speak two or three, and let the other judge. If anything be revealed to another that sitteth by, let the first hold his peace. For ye all may be comforted, and the spirits of the prophets are subject to the prophets."

When we began ministry, I spent several days at the local Christian bookstore seeking for the Bible God wanted me to use to teach the people and build the ministry. Finally, with the help of one of the Bible consultants,

I made a decision to purchase one that had 77 articles covering everything I needed to teach. I thought we were a Full Gospel Ministry, but when I began to teach on the prophetic, I realized that I was already exercising the gift through the anointing. Through the leading of the Holy Spirit, the gift of the prophetic was released and activated to those who felt the unction. I had received many prophecies before we started the ministry, and as we continued to build some of those prophecies were being manifested. I was ready to embrace all that God was doing to confirm the call to ministry, so the prophetic thrusted the ministry to begin to see great breakthrough, deliverance, favor, signs and wonders. In 2000, I met Apostle John Eckhardt at a conference in Michigan. He sent his prophetic team who confirmed our prophetic ministry was already activated.

Prophecy is "the yielding of your voice to hear from God and speaking the Word of the Lord." All believers should have this unction by faith. Then there is the gift of prophecy that can be stirred up. 2 Timothy 1:6, "Therefore I remind you to stir up the gift of God which is in you through the laying on of hands. This gift is for those whose prophecy brings edification, exhortation and comfort, 1 Corinthians 14:3. The office of the prophet is the highest level in the prophetic realm because they prophesy with more authority and revelation. The office of the prophet is graced to carry corrections, confirmations, impartations, activations bringing clarity to the move of God. Prophets are like a vacuum cleaner to the church. They dig deep, expose and get rid of all that is not like God. Apostles and prophets fit together like a hand in a glove to bring apostolic ministry into the full advancement of the kingdom.

Praise Assembly has a company of prophets who brings true authenticity to the restoration of Prophetic Ministry. The teaching on the prophetic has been essential in keeping the prophets encouraged and having more passion to see the prophecies come to pass. For more teaching on the prophetic, I recommend *God Still Speaks* by John Eckhardt.

Apostolic Team

Apostolic teams consist of apostles and five-fold ministry gifts who are sent out into nations, churches, and regions to build apostolic ministries. The team releases new revelation of truths, prophetic insights and the operations of the gifts for miracles and healings through preaching and teaching. They are led by an apostle who is called and anointed to build apostolically throughout regions and nations networking apostolic churches. These apostles and teams have built a paradigm model locally and now have a heart to meet the needs of the many pastors who know there is more for them and the people, but don't know how to get there. The apostolic teams are to provide the necessary equipping of the local leadership, so they can break through the old way of doing church into strong governing apostolic ministries, being effective in every area for the spiritual growth of the people. The team should bring refreshing, revival, revelation and impartation to the churches that they are being sent to. Pastors who are ready to move beyond the old because they had an apostolic encounter will need to pray and be sure they are ready for an apostolic team to come and impart because that impartation brings on an accountability to them and their people that all things will become new. The mission, the mindset, the vision, the lives of the people will have to change. No longer will there be church-minded people, but kingdom-minded where the kingdom of God is being advanced as a lifestyle. Pastors must connect to the apostolic team in order to have continuous impartation to bring total manifestation of an apostolic church in the areas of praise and worship, deliverance, prophecy, warfare prayer, prosperity, love, faith, and evangelism. The apostolic team will help perfect the saints. Ephesians 4, "There is a Macedonian call throughout the earth for the apostolic team to help build the end-time ministry."

Acts 16:9, 10, "And a vision appeared to Paul in the night; there stood a man of Macedonia, and prayed him, saying, Come over into Macedonia, and help us. And after he had seen the vision, immediately we endeavored to go into Macedonia, assuredly gathering that the Lord had called us for to reach the gospel unto them." The anointing that has been imparted through the team must be continued, so the local pastor should be humble and submissive to the spirit of God to make a divine connection for the sake of building the people so they can identify their gifts and calling.

The Impact Apostolic Team of Praise Assembly Apostolic Faith Ministries International was birthed out of my being called to preach at women's conferences and taking a team of people that I thought were just supporters, but as we had already developed a strong prophetic and deliverance ministry, God would use me in a totally different way through praise, exhortation and preaching so that there was always an explosive move of God, where people were getting delivered and filled with the Holy Ghost, realizing there was more. There was a prophetic word released to me that said more than once, "Apostle, you are the apostle of the apostles." So as time passed, the mandate was established with calls from pastors who were ready to transition from a pastoral paradigm to an apostolic paradigm.

After years of building, but not yet confirmed, as a team, at a conference in Louisiana with Pastor Georgia Williams, I met a Filipino lady named Vickie from California whose life was changed overnight. She called me and invited me to go to the Philippines and preach. She arranged everything, and thirteen of us went to Cebu and three other territories. I ministered twelve times in eight days, and we saw the most powerful manifestation that it is unexplainable, but confirmation was certain that God was developing a work that was going to make a global impact to restore the ministry of the Apostolic. One of the churches, which was held in a movie theater, was not on our schedule, but the pastor asked for me to come and minister. I had 30 minutes to preach. It was time for the movie to open, and the pastor and his elders were still on the concrete floor. Getting up drunk in the spirit, they invited us to lunch. Later we met with 33 of those who sensed the prophetic, and me and my team activated them. We formed a relationship even on our return. The pastor had been looking for an apostle who would cover what he already believed was an Apostolic Ministry. Several months later, I took the Apostolic Team back, and we did a paradigm shift and an ordination service. One of the young pastors has since established an apostolic church in Cebu and named it Praise Assembly. This was my confirmation that we were an Apostolic Team Ministry, divinely revealing it to us first, and we have continued traveling and working as a team to fulfill purpose and destiny for the churches as well the team.

Apostolic Covenant Connection

An apostle has the ability to form apostolic relationships. They form covenant relationship with pastors who they have been divinely connected to by the spirit. This covenant provides the place and process for spiritual fathering/mothering so that true spiritual sons and daughters can be raised up. This process is an apostolic function for those to whom the apostle wants to help by teaching the Apostolic Ministry. The Holy Spirit places apostles into meaningful relationship with helping pave the way for apostolic succession and transference of the mantle and ministry gifts. These connections are usually developed out of being called to minister in different conferences. The covenant is divinely connected between a seasoned functioning apostle and a pastor who is ready to transition to the Apostolic Ministry. These emerging pastors are willing to receive the teaching and training of the apostle in every area of ministry.

God has released me and the Apostolic Team in a ministry of Apostolic Leadership Paradigm Shift. Our mandate is to help pastors to transition into Apostolic Ministries. This transition requires gaining a relationship of trust, love, commitment and friendship. After the pastors decide they are ready for the transition, and they've received confirmation that they want to shift, we begin a relationship, both spiritual and personal. I have made covenant with pastors from all around the world, and in the spiritual bonding, have helped them to make total transformation of their ministry. My commitment to them has connected us not only with me as their apostle, but also as their spiritual mother. In this relationship, I provide protection and covering for their lives and ministries. I work directly with them to meet their needs as well as visit their churches periodically. Also, I make weekly contact with them with a covenant conference call, releasing apostolic impartation and strategies and to keep them encouraged as they continue to transition to functioning in the Apostolic Ministry.

Praise Assembly Apostolic Faith Ministries International serves as the "apostolic hub" where all covenant connected sons and daughters gather to receive Apostolic/Prophetic impartation, activation, and release of more revelation that is needed to fulfill their callings and destinies every September as well as a

Passion to Pursue Purpose Family Conference which is an awesome gathering and a time of releasing of Destiny and Purpose.

I thank God for my Divine Covenant Connection sons and daughters for entrusting the Apostolic Mandate on my life that has been confirmed with manifestation of the reformation of their ministries. All of them have been divinely connected by God because what God has ordained and covenant connected, He will cover and sustain.

Apostle Fannie Wallace has set a Paradigm for many leaders through apostolic demonstration and manifestation of the validity of shifting from a pastoral mindset into an apostolic mindset. With this shifting of many leaders she has established a Divine Covenant connection of sons and daughters to train them to function and build strong apostolic ministries. she is a global Apostle of Apostles with a mandate to bring change to the body of Christ.

For information contact:

Shanda Glover
Praise Assembly Apostolic Faith Ministries Int'l.
1-45-677-3553
Website: www.paafmi.org

Made in the USA
San Bernardino, CA
21 March 2014